Destination Detectives

China

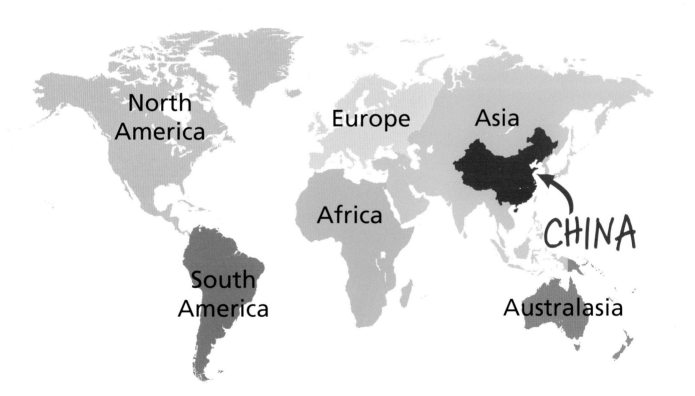

North
America

Europe

Asia

Africa

South
America

CHINA

Australasia

Ali Brownlie Bojang

Produced for Raintree by
White-Thomson Publishing Ltd,
Bridgewater Business Centre,
210 High Street, Lewes, BN7 2NH

First published in Great Britain by Raintree,
Halley Court, Jordan Hill, Oxford OX2 8EJ,
Part of Harcourt Education.
Raintree is a registered trademark of
Harcourt Education Ltd.

Editorial: Sonya Newland, Melanie Waldron and Lucy Beevor
Design: Gary Frost
Picture Research: Amy Sparks
Production: Chloe Bloom

Originated by Modern Age
Printed and bound in China
By South China Printing Company

10 digit ISBN 1406203068
13 digit ISBN 9781406203066
10 9 8 7 6 5 4 3 2 1
11 10 09 08 07 06

British Library Cataloguing in Publication Data
Brownlie Bojang, Ali, 1949–
    China. - (Destination Detective)
    1. China - Geography - Juvenile literature 2. China -
    Social life and customs - 21st century - Juvenile literature
    3. China - Civilisation - Juvenile literature
    I. Title
    951'.06

Acknowledgements
The Art Archive pp. 17 (William Sewell); Corbis pp. 9
(Reuters), 10 (Keren Su), 13 (Xinhua), 15t (Royal Ontario
Museum), 28 (Ron Watts), 29 (Keren Su), 33 (Chi
Haifeng/Xinhua), 38 (Michael S. Yamashita), 38–39 (Vince
Streano), 42 (Wang Jianmin/Xinhua Photos); Photolibrary
pp. 4–5 (Pacific Stock), 7 (IFA-Bilderteam Gmbh), 10–11
(Panorama Stock Photo), 12 (Panorama Stock Photo), 15b
(Pacific Stock), 19 (Index Stock Imagery), 20–21 (Panorama
Stock Photo), 21 (Panorama Stock Photo), 24 (Panorama
Stock Photo), 27 (Panorama Stock Photo), 31 (Panorama
Stock Photo), 34 (Botanica), 35 (Pacific Stock), 37, 40
(Daniel Cox), 41 (IFA-Bilderteam Gmbh), 43r (Panorama
Stock Photo); TopFoto pp. 16 (Nathan Strange/uppa.co.uk),
23r (Uppa Ltd), 25 (Image Works), 39; WTPix pp. 5t, 5m,
5b, 6, 8, 14, 18, 22, 23l, 26t, 26b, 30, 32, 36, 43l.

Cover photograph of lion dance reproduced with permission
of Panorama Stock Photo Co., Ltd/OSF/Photolibrary.

Thanks to Luo Jailing and Simon Scoones.

Every effort has been made to contact copyright
holders of any material reproduced in this book.
Any omissions will be rectified in subsequent
printings if notice is given to the publishers.

The paper used to print this book comes from
sustainable resources.

Contents

Where in the world? 4

So this is China! 6

Climate & landscape 10

A bit of history 14

Getting around 18

City life 20

Life in the countryside 28

People & culture. 34

Wildlife & environment. 40

Stay or go? 42

Find out more 44

China – facts & figures 46

Glossary 47

Index. 48

Any words appearing in the text in bold, **like this,** are explained in the glossary. You can also look out for them in the Word Bank box at the bottom of each page.

Where in the world?

The middle of the world

Zhong Guo is the **Mandarin** word for China – it means "middle or centre kingdom". The ancient Chinese people believed that they were at the centre of the world, and that the Temple of Heaven in Beijing was the centre of China.

You are being chased by a dancing dragon spitting fire. Suddenly you hear a loud bang and the dragon runs away. You wake with a start and realize that you have been dreaming. There is a lot of noise outside. You look out of the hotel window and see children laughing and shouting as they watch firecrackers going off. It's almost midnight. People start to count down: "Four, three, two, one! *Xin nian yu kuai*! Happy New Year!" Fireworks light up the sky.

Lion dances are performed at New Year celebrations. They are believed to ward off demons and bring good luck in the coming year.

WORD BANK   Mandarin official language of China

It is the Chinese New Year, and everywhere children are showing off their new clothes and counting the pocket money they have received to mark the occasion. New Year celebrations start sometime between 30 January and 20 February with the new moon, and end on the full moon fifteen days later. This is a noisy and colourful introduction to your journey around China – and Beijing, the capital of China, is your starting point.

Find out later...

Where is the world's largest palace?

What was this huge wall built for?

What type of exercise are these people doing?

So this is China!

China at a glance

SIZE:
9.59 million square kilometres (3.7 million square miles)

CAPITAL:
Beijing

POPULATION:
1.3 billion

RELIGION:
Confucianism, Buddhism, Taoism (see pages 38 and 39)

OFFICIAL LANGUAGE:
Chinese **Mandarin**

CURRENCY:
Yuan RMB (RMB stands for *renminbi*, which means "people's currency")

TYPE OF GOVERNMENT:
Communist republic (ruled by one political party – the Chinese Communist Party)

You notice a map of China on the wall. You can see that it is a huge, irregular-shaped country. It is only slightly smaller than the United States, and two and a half times the size of Western Europe. Someone has been here before you and stuck labels on the map.

Unusually shaped **limestone** hills are found in the southern **provinces** of Yunnan and Guizhou. This is known as karst scenery.

The Chang Jiang River is 6,380 kilometres (3,987 miles) long – roughly the distance from London, UK, to New Delhi in India, or from Seattle to Chicago and back! It is the third-longest river in the world. It runs from the mountains in the west to the East China Sea.

WORD BANK   **autonomous**   being separate or able to govern a region independently
limestone   rock created from the remains of sea animals

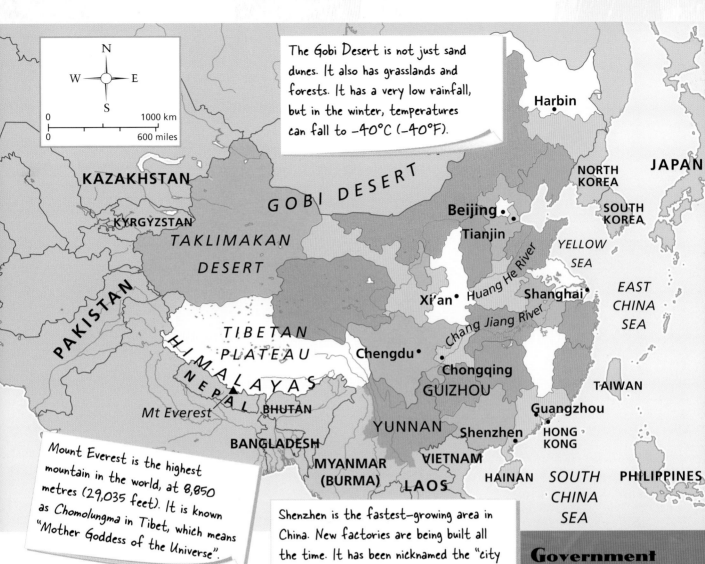

The Gobi Desert is not just sand dunes. It also has grasslands and forests. It has a very low rainfall, but in the winter, temperatures can fall to -40°C (-40°F).

Harbin

KAZAKHSTAN

GOBI DESERT

JAPAN

NORTH KOREA

KYRGYZSTAN

SOUTH KOREA

TAKLIMAKAN DESERT

Beijing

Tianjin

YELLOW SEA

Huang He River

Xi'an

EAST CHINA SEA

Shanghai

PAKISTAN

TIBETAN PLATEAU

HIMALAYAS

NEPAL

Mt Everest

BHUTAN

Chang Jiang River

Chengdu

Chongqing

GUIZHOU

YUNNAN

Guangzhou

TAIWAN

Shenzhen

HONG KONG

BANGLADESH

MYANMAR (BURMA)

LAOS

VIETNAM

HAINAN

SOUTH CHINA SEA

PHILIPPINES

Mount Everest is the highest mountain in the world, at 8,850 metres (29,035 feet). It is known as Chomolungma in Tibet, which means "Mother Goddess of the Universe".

Shenzhen is the fastest-growing area in China. New factories are being built all the time. It has been nicknamed the "city of overnight growth". 75 percent of the world's toys are made here.

The yak's thick coat helps it survive the low temperatures of Tibet.

Government in China

China's local government is divided into 22 provinces, two Special Administrative Regions (Hong Kong and Macau), and four **municipalities** (Shanghai, Beijing, Chongqing, and Tianjin). It also has five areas that are allowed a certain level of self-rule – called **autonomous** regions.

municipalities main cities in China that have the same status as provinces
province region that has its own local government

Exploring Beijing

The next morning you wake early and make your way to the centre of Beijing. You find yourself surrounded by buildings and open spaces. Emperors and **peasants** alike have lived and visited here for thousands of years.

You walk across the vast space of Tiananmen Square. This is a popular meeting place for the people of Beijing. Thousands gathered here in 1949 to celebrate the founding of their new country – the People's Republic of China. In 1989, hundreds of students were killed by soldiers while on their way to the Square to demonstrate for more freedom from the Government's strict laws. Today it is full of young children flying kites and tourists making their way to the Forbidden City.

The Forbidden City

The Forbidden City is known as *Gu Gong* in Chinese and was the home of emperors for hundreds of years. Building began in 1406 and it was completed fourteen years later. It is the world's largest palace, covering 74 hectares (183 acres).

Tiananmen Square

Tiananmen Square is one of the largest public spaces in the world. At 440,000 square metres (4.7 million square feet), it is big enough to hold half a million people.

The Forbidden City is now one of the most popular tourist attractions in the world.

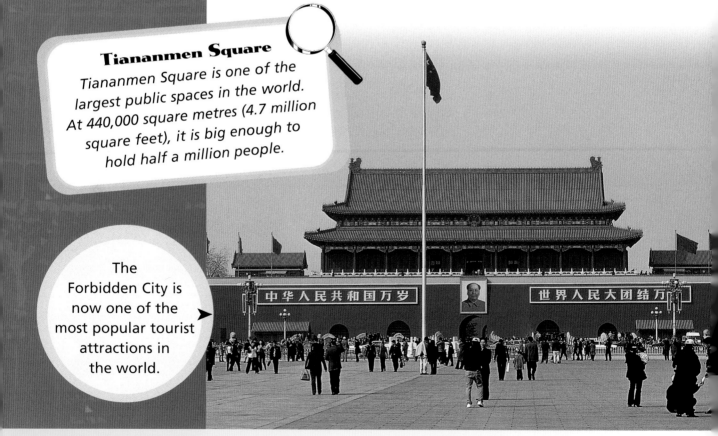

WORD BANK   peasants poor people who lived and worked off the land

Desert winds

Looking up at the sky you notice that a yellow cloud has blocked out the sun. A wind is starting to blow and the children are having trouble holding on to their kites. High winds from the Taklimakan Desert in the west are bringing clouds of choking sand to the capital city. People have difficulty breathing and many wear masks. Drivers cannot see where they are going. The Government is building a wall of trees north of the city to try to prevent future sandstorms affecting Beijing.

Olympics 2008

As part of its preparations for the 2008 Olympics, Beijing expanded its airport, developed a high-speed railway, built a new sewage-treatment plant, and improved the city lighting.

Beijing's traffic crawls through a sandstorm. The winds can reach up to 70 kilometres (44 miles) per hour, and the swirling sand makes it difficult to see.

Climate & landscape

China is so huge that the **climate** and scenery change dramatically between different regions. It ranges from bitterly cold in the northern winters to unbearably hot in the southern summers. It has a "north **drought** and south flood" climate pattern. In other words, there is not enough rain in the north and too much in the south.

Beijing winter

In Beijing the climate is hot in summer but cold in winter. When it snows, people come out of their houses with brooms and sweep the snow away from the streets. If you decide to come back here you'll need to bring some warm clothes. The wind blows straight from the coldest place on Earth – Siberia.

In the northern city of Harbin, winters are so cold that people are able to build giant sculptures made out of snow.

WORD BANK   **drought** temporary shortage of water
dynasty series of rulers from the same family

In the north the summers are warm – and can be hot – but the winters are very cold. In contrast, the south has a **tropical** climate. Winters are warm and summers are hot and humid. During the summer, **typhoons** often happen and can cause terrible devastation. During these violent storms, winds can reach speeds of 120 kilometres (74 miles) per hour. In September 2005, the most powerful typhoon in 30 years hit southern China, and thousands of people had to be evacuated from villages along the coast.

Temperature extremes

	Minimum	Maximum
Beijing	-20°C (-4°F)	38°C (100°F)
Turpan	-10°C (14°F)	47°C (117°F)
Lhasa	-16°C (3°F)	29°C (84°F)
Guangzhou	1°C (34°F)	38°C (100°F)

Skiing

The long, cold winters and the mountains in Manchuria, to the north of Beijing, make ideal conditions for skiing. China's largest ski resort, at Yabuli, used to be a royal hunting ground in the Qing **dynasty**. The emperors used to hunt tigers and bears here.

Families enjoy a day out on one of Shenzhen's tropical beaches in southern China.

Equator imaginary line around Earth
tropical anything to do with the region either side of the **Equator**

The Chang Jiang

Chinese people call the Chang Jiang the "Mother River", because its water helps produce the crops that feed the population. In some years, however, it brings floods that can cause much destruction of homes and farmland.

Highlands and lowlands

To the west and the south of China lies the huge Tibetan **Plateau**, which covers over one-third of the country. This is a very rugged area. It is difficult to live here because of the harsh **terrain** and cold **climate**. Along the plateau's southern edge lie the Himalayas, the highest mountain range in the world.

To the east lie the main lowland **floodplains**, formed by **fertile silt** and soil left by the rivers. China's two main rivers are the Chang Jiang (Yangtze River) and the Huang He (Yellow River). The rivers are important ways of transporting goods between the east and west of the country, especially bulky materials like coal. These floodplains are China's main farming areas and where most people live.

On the Tibetan Plateau, movements in the earth have created large rock formations (seen at the bottom here), known as "clay forests".

WORD BANK   floodplain area that floods when river water rises
silt fine particles of sand and rock carried and then deposited by a river

The Three Gorges Dam

A huge dam is being built on the Chang Jiang river, due to be completed in 2009. It will allow ships to travel as far as Chongqing, bringing more business and jobs. The force of the water will be used to power

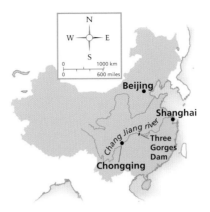

turbines that will produce electricity. The dam will control the river and help stop the terrible flooding that has killed over one million people in the last 100 years. However, many people are worried that this project will damage the environment, and drown towns and villages when the reservoir fills with water. What will happen to all the people who will have to move?

The Dam project

The Three Gorges Dam will be 185 metres (606 feet) high and 1,981 metres (6,500 feet) broad. The power plant will supply up to 15 percent of China's energy. It will flood and cover thirteen cities, 140 towns, 1,340 villages, and 30,000 hectares (74,130 acres) of farmland. 1.3 million people will have to move from their homes.

When completed, the Three Gorges Dam will be the largest **hydroelectric** dam in the world.

terrain an area of land
turbine engine powered by water, steam, gas, or air

A bit of history

You decide to continue your exploration of Beijing by visiting the Imperial Palace. This is just one of the many museums that show visitors to the city what China was like in the past.

Chinese dynasties

For thousands of years, the Chinese people – nearly all of them poor **peasants** – were ruled by a series of different families, known as **dynasties**. Each dynasty is remembered for something special. For example, during the Xia dynasty – around 4,000 years ago – writing was invented. During the Qin dynasty, around 200 BC, a series of smaller walls began to be joined together to make the Great Wall of China. This huge wall was meant to keep out attackers from the north, but it was not completed until the 15th century, nearly 1,600 years later.

An inventive nation

Many inventions have come from China. These include paper and printing, fireworks and **gunpowder**, the wheelbarrow, kites, and the compass. Kites were used in wartime to send messages to prisoners. Sometimes they were made to create strange sounds and flown over the enemy to put them off.

The Great Wall of China was built out of granite, stone, brick, and earth. It stretches for 6,350 kilometres (3,946 miles) across northern China.

WORD BANK   BC stands for "Before Christ"

The Ming dynasty (1368–1644) is famous for producing beautiful pots and vases. This is why we now call such things "china". The Ming dynasty is also remembered for being very powerful and sometimes very brutal and cruel towards the peasants.

A camel caravan sets out along the Silk Road in the Taklimakan Desert.

Beautiful porcelain vases from the Ming and Qing dynasties. These are all over 300 years old and worth a great deal of money!

The Silk Road

The Silk Road was a route that connected China to the Middle East and Europe through deserts and mountains. People have been using the Silk Road for more than 2,000 years. Goods were traded along the way – from China there was silk, herbal medicines, bamboo, paper, and gunpowder, and from the West, gold, grapes, and rugs.

The Communist republic

By the beginning of the 20th century, many Chinese people were fed up with their rulers, the emperors. The people had put up with many natural disasters such as floods, earthquakes, and famine. They felt that the rulers had done nothing to help them.

In 1934, a man named Mao Zedong, the leader of the **Communists**, led his supporters – known as the Red Army – on a long journey across China to escape from their enemies. This became known as "The Long March", as it took 370 days. Along the way, many more people joined the march. In 1949, Mao became China's leader and the country became a Communist republic. The state looked after its people "from the cradle to the grave", and China had little to do with other countries.

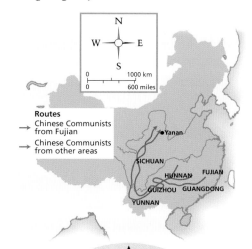

Routes
→ Chinese Communists from Fujian
→ Chinese Communists from other areas

During "The Long March", Mao and his supporters travelled 8,000 kilometres (4,960 miles) from the south to the north of China.

A copy of the "Little Red Book", with a picture of the Chinese leader, Mao Zedong.

Communist person who follows a political belief system that calls for a classless society, where nobody owns anything and resources belong to a community

China changes

After Mao died in 1976, the new leaders decided that China needed to do more business with the rest of the world. Many new factories were built, often with money from foreigners. Goods can now be produced in China cheaper than anywhere else in the world, because people work for low wages. This makes a lot of money for the country. Some people are much better off, but millions are still very poor, especially those working in the factories.

Hu Jintao

In March 2003, Hu Jintao became the President of China and continued the country's **reforms**. He comes from Anhui **Province** and enjoys table tennis and ballroom dancing.

The Four Modernizations

In 1975, Dong Xiaoping, then leader of China, introduced the "Four Modernizations". This was a plan to increase production and **manufacturing**. It was the beginning of the huge changes China has gone through in the last 30 years.

A poster from 1949, showing crowds in Tiananmen Square celebrating the founding of the new Chinese republic.

manufacturing making things from raw materials
reform change made by the Government to improve the country

Getting around

Already you are fascinated by China, and you can't wait to begin exploring the different regions. You need to find out how to get around this huge country.

Because China is so big, the quickest way of seeing the different areas is to travel by plane. The national airline, Air China, flies to more than 100 cities. However, flying is an expensive way to travel, and most Chinese people cannot afford it. Many people travel by train or bus instead. These are often very crowded, especially during national holidays when everyone is travelling to be with their families. Some long-distance buses show films to help pass the time.

Rail travel

The train from Beijing to Hong Kong takes 24 hours. You can choose whether to sit all the way or sleep in a bunk bed. The cabins usually have four beds. A washroom is shared between all the passengers in the carriage.

The Trans-Siberian Railway

You can go all the way to China from London, UK, or Paris, France, by train. The Trans-Siberian Railway takes nine days and you have to change trains three times.

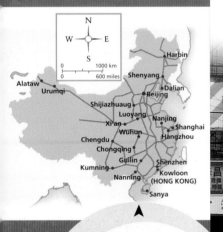

China has an extensive railway network, and more lines are being built, particularly in the south-west.

These buses are hurrying people to work in Kowloon, Hong Kong.

Bikes and cars

All over China, apart from in the very hilly places like Chongqing, you can see people getting around on bicycles. It is estimated that there are more than 300 million bicycles in China.

Over the last few years, some people have become richer, and have bought their own cars. In large cities like Beijing and Shanghai, new roads are being built all the time to try to deal with the increasing number of cars.

Underground trains
Shanghai, Beijing, Hong Kong, Guangzhou, and Tianjin all have their own underground rail system or subway.

Car boom
Over 2.2 million cars were sold in China in 2004. This was nearly 14 percent more than in the previous year. People are buying cars in China faster than anywhere else in the world. However, only three in every 1,000 Chinese people own a car today.

These cyclists are waiting for the traffic lights to change. Bicycles are an important way of getting around in China's towns and cities.

City life

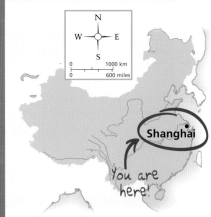

You decide to go to Shanghai, the largest city in China, to find out more about life in China's **urban** areas. You book a sleeper – a bunk bed on the train – as the journey takes twelve hours and travels through the night. You jump on the train at Beijing station at 7 p.m. and arrive at Shanghai railway station in Puxi at 7 a.m. the following morning.

Booming Shanghai

You make your way to the ferry that will take you to the Pudong area of Shanghai. The boat is crammed with bikes and scooters, and you push your way through to the stall that sells five-spice eggs – spicy scrambled eggs. These are a Chinese speciality, which you buy for your breakfast.

Pudong

Pudong is the new part of Shanghai, and has been built since 1990. It is the main trade and financial centre, and lies on the other side of the Huangpu River from old Shanghai. Bridges, tunnels, and a ferry connect the two areas.

The ultra-modern skyline of Pudong in Shanghai, showing the Oriental Pearl Tower, which is 468 metres (1,536 feet) high.

WORD BANK   metro rail system in an urban area

For an amazing view of the city you go to the top of the Oriental Pearl TV Tower. Below you is a city of 13 million people. You can hear the roar of bulldozers and the pounding of hammers on hundreds of buildings sites far below. New hotels, office blocks, and roads are all being built here. Shanghai is typical of how China's cities are rapidly changing.

The Maglev train can take passengers the 30 kilometres (19 miles) from downtown Shanghai to the airport at Pudong in just eight minutes.

Great heights

The Shanghai World Financial Centre will be one of the tallest buildings in the world when it is finished, at 492 metres (1,614 feet).

The magical Maglev

The Maglev is Shanghai's new **metro** train. It works by using very powerful magnets that lift the entire train 10 millimetres (0.4 inches) above a special track. It has no driver, causes no pollution, and can travel at speeds of up to 435 kilometres (270 miles) per hour.

urban relating to a city or built-up area

Shanghai and Beijing have really impressed you. They have shown you some of China's ancient past, as well as how modern and lively Chinese cities can be. So what is it like to live here? You decide to find out how people start their day.

Early-morning exercise

You get up early and take the **metro** to Jing An Park. It is 6 a.m. and already there are lines of people doing slow, controlled exercises and **meditating**. They are doing Tai Chi, a traditional Chinese form of exercise involving a series of slow body movements.

There are some old men sitting on folding chairs at easels, painting Chinese characters. One of them offers you his brush for you to have a go! Sometimes the artists get up and join in with the exercises.

Rush-hour in Shanghai

By 7.30 a.m. everyone has finished exercising, and the pavements are full of people rushing to work or school. Nearly everyone is wearing Western clothes and has a mobile phone, usually worn on a strap hanging from their neck. The buses are beginning to fill up. Some people are hailing taxis.

Tai Chi is one of the Chinese **martial arts**. It exercises the mind as well as the body.

Calligraphy artists are believed to live long lives.

Calligraphy

Chinese calligraphy dates back thousands of years. It is a form of art where Chinese characters are painted as a way of expressing how you feel, to help you concentrate and to relax.

Shopping has become a popular pastime in China's big cities. This is a crowded street in Shanghai.

meditating method of concentrating to calm the mind and body

Leisure time

People in cities have more leisure time now than they used to have. Shopping in the new modern malls, eating out, or going to clubs and discos are popular ways of relaxing. Many people still enjoy the traditional Chinese Opera. These are musical dramas that involve mock fighting and acrobatics. The actors paint their faces and wear colourful costumes. Younger people are more interested in pop singers such as Cui Jian. He plays rock, techno, and hip-hop music to crowds all over the country.

A bustling modern indoor shopping mall in Shanghai. ▶

24

Hutongs

In most of China's cities, big changes are taking place and many people are benefiting. There are some disadvantages to this fast progress, though. Many old buildings are being torn down to make way for new ones. The *hutongs* of Beijing are old houses built close together around a small courtyard. These are disappearing fast to make way for apartment blocks and wider roads. This means that the traditional close community life, where everyone knows one another, is slowly disappearing.

City facts

- More than 500 million Chinese people live in cities.
- There are nearly 700 cities in China altogether.
- There are eleven cities in China that have a population of over two million.
- China's big cities lie in the east. There is no city in the west of the country with a population of more than one million.

A gateway leading into an old *hutong* in Beijing.

You have a look in a guidebook to see which other cities in China are worth visiting.

Hong Kong

The United Kingdom took control of Hong Kong from the Chinese after the countries were at war between 1839 and 1842. In 1997, the United Kingdom handed it back. From a small fishing village, it has grown to be the world's fourth-largest banking and financial centre.

A fish market in Hong Kong.

Seaports

China's 18,000-kilometre (11,250-mile) coastline has been described as the busiest in the world. Most of China's **manufactured** goods are taken to many different countries by ship from its seaports. The main **ports** are Shanghai, Shenzhen, Hong Kong, Guangzhou, and Tianjin.

Hong Kong is a busy, exciting city, with a mix of traditional Chinese life and modern Western businesses.

Harbin

Harbin is a thriving industrial city in the north. Its buildings look Russian, as many of them were built at the time when Harbin was a stop on the rail journey from Russia.

Guangzhou

Guangzhou is a very old city, dating back nearly 3,000 years. It is now at the heart of a rapidly growing manufacturing area.

Xi'an

Xi'an is one of the world's four major ancient cities, along with Athens (Greece), Cairo (Egypt), and Rome (Italy). It lies at the western end of the Silk Road.

Chengdu

Chengdu is believed to be the cleanest city in China. It is famous for its parks and hibiscus flowers. It lies in the middle of some of China's most **fertile** land, and its markets are always full of fresh vegetables and fruits.

The world's Chinatowns

Many cities across the world have their own "Chinatown", where you can find Chinese restaurants, shops, theatres, and cinemas. These include New York, Chicago, and San Francisco in the United States, London and Manchester in the United Kingdom, and Sydney and Melbourne in Australia.

Chengdu has a population of 10 million, and a history dating back 2,300 years.

Life in the countryside

Paddy fields

Growing rice needs a lot of care and a lot of people. The fields – known as paddies – are flooded with water, as rice needs this to grow. Each plant is sown by hand in the soft soil. The fields need constant weeding before the rice is harvested. It is back-breaking work.

You are now keen to move on and see more of China. You pack your bag and jump on a bus, leaving the city far behind. You gaze out of the window and see villages and fields rolling by. You notice a man walking behind a plough being pulled by a buffalo. It is all very different from the hustle and bustle of the city.

Farming

Farming is very important in China, as it provides food for the country's huge population. China is **self-sufficient** in food. Mostly people and animals do the work rather than machines, but every day more and more farmers are using tractors and other machines. This is increasing the amount of food they can produce.

A farmer ploughs his rice field.

WORD BANK arable land that is suitable for cultivation
growing season period when it is warm enough for crops to grow

In hilly areas, farmers have learnt how to use every bit of land possible to grow their crops. **Terraces** follow the **contours** of the hills, making it possible to grow crops just about anywhere. Some of the terraced fields are over 700 years old.

In the north there is a short **growing season** and water is in short supply. In the south, the warm **climate** allows farmers to have two or sometimes three crops a year.

Fast fact

China has 23 percent of the world's population. It feeds this from only about seven percent of the world's **arable** land.

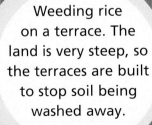

Weeding rice on a terrace. The land is very steep, so the terraces are built to stop soil being washed away.

self-sufficient able to produce enough food for the population
terrace step or ledge cut into a hillside

Village life

You get off the bus just outside a small village and walk down the wide main street. There are old people sitting around a table playing mah jong, a game where you build walls with tiles. Mah jong is popular with people all over China.

Many young people have left the village to find work elsewhere. Most of the families in the village rely on the money these young people send home. Most Chinese people – about 64 percent – still live in the countryside, although this percentage is getting less and less each year, as people leave to find work in the cities. To improve life for people in the countryside, the Government is rebuilding old schools and providing electricity and safe drinking water in areas that do not already have them.

A farmer and his wife take their produce to market.

Courtyard homes

You decide to have a look around one of the houses. It stands in a courtyard, where hens peck at the dirt and pigs grunt in the corner. Rice has been scattered at the far end to dry in the sun. The yard is surrounded by houses. The man who lives here is head of the family, so his house faces south and gets the most sunshine – the most favoured position – while the other houses are occupied by his grown-up children and his brother's family.

China's villages

There are more than 700,000 villages in China, most of them based on farming. They are usually small, with around 200 to 500 inhabitants.

Ancient architecture

Many villages in China are hundreds of years old. These are now being **preserved** as special examples of Chinese architecture. They have become popular tourist attractions. Some of them have been used for filming movies such as the 2000 film *Crouching Tiger, Hidden Dragon*.

Children play around the entrance to a courtyard in a country village.

Inside a courtyard home

Like most of the other houses in the village, this one has electricity and there is a small black-and-white television. There is no running water, though. The children of the family fetch water from a nearby well. Life in villages like this has not changed much in the past 100 years.

Inside the house, a table is laden with dishes of rice, noodles, pork, chicken, and vegetables, all grown or raised in the country. The family invites you to join them, and you tuck in with your chopsticks.

Village schools

In the villages, children start school when they are six and stay there for nine years. If they want to go to a Junior High School, they have to pass an exam.

Television

Over 96 percent of the population has access to a television. There are over 50 channels, covering news, sport, films, and shopping channels. One of the most popular programmes is a chat show hosted by Chen Luyu – China's version of Oprah Winfrey.

Three boys on their way to school in rural China.

They know they will have to work very hard towards this. Chinese children learn subjects similar to those taught in Western schools, but there is one big difference – Chinese children have to learn Chinese characters off by heart. This is much more difficult than learning the alphabet.

Many children in **rural** areas leave school early because they need to help their families with the farming.

雨 木

Chinese characters often look like the words they represent. These are the characters for "rain" and "tree".

Schools like this one, in rural areas, receive less Government **funding** than those in the towns and cities.

Schooling in China

Many schools in rural areas lack enough teachers and up-to-date books. They receive less money from the Government than schools in the cities. On average 44.3 yuan (£3.11) is spent on primary-school students in cities, but only 28.12 yuan (£1.98) is spent on every rural student.

rural relating to the countryside

People & culture

You have met many people on your travels so far, but there are over a billion people in China, and there are lots of differences between them.

The people of China

There are 56 different **ethnic groups** in China. Each group has its own language and traditions, although everyone learns **Mandarin** at school. The Han is by far the largest group, making up about 90 percent of China's people. They are found everywhere in China, but most live in the low-lying areas in the east. The second-largest ethnic group is the Zhuang. There are around 18 million Zhuang in China – nearly as many as the population of Australia!

Shrinking families

In order to prevent the population becoming too large, the Government encourages most families to have only one child. This does not apply to some minority ethnic groups or people living in **rural** areas, who need children to work on the farms.

China's main minority groups

Ethnic Group	Population
Zhuang	18 million
Manchu	9.8 million
Mongolian	4.8 million
Tibetan	4.6 million

> ▶ Some Chinese people are only allowed to have one child.

Some of the larger ethnic groups live in the border regions in the west and north. The Chinese Government has given them more power to rule themselves. For example, the Uygur and the Tibetans have their own **autonomous** regions.

Chinese customs

- Chinese people do not like to say "no" or to say that they don't understand something. This can be very confusing!

- If someone gives you a present, stand up and accept it with both hands. Do not open it straight away.

- When visiting someone, always take a small gift for them – like flowers or some chocolates.

Tibetans are one of China's main ethnic groups. These girls are wearing traditional Tibetan dress, which is very colourful, with beads and necklaces.

Sport

The Chinese are a sport-loving nation. To find out more about this and Chinese culture, you travel back to Beijing.

Soccer has become hugely popular, and Chinese people follow the teams in the English Premier League. You join some Chinese friends and go to watch a match in the Worker's Stadium. People shout slogans and wave their red flags as the Chinese side beats the opposition. Other popular sports include gymnastics, table tennis, and tennis.

Chinese sports

China has introduced many sports to the rest of the world, including archery, polo, and wrestling.

The Chinese enjoy many different sports. Here, a group of young men play basketball in a city park.

Food

There is a wide variety of food to choose from all the different regions of China. Rice is the main food, although around Beijing and the north people eat more bread and noodles. In Sichuan people use a lot of chilli in their cooking, and it can be hot enough to burn your mouth unless you are used to it.

Fish is an important part of their diet for many Chinese people. It is often eaten on New Year's Eve, as it is thought to bring wealth and prosperity. There are over 150 different species of fish in the seas and rivers, including hairtail, chub mackerel, herring, octopus, and squid. Fish are also bred in ponds and lakes inland.

In the cities you can get any kind of food you want – from hamburgers and pizza to duck's foot.

China tea

Legend has it that tea was discovered when some leaves blew into the Chinese emperor's cup of hot water in 2737 BC. China produces several different kinds of tea, including strong Gunpowder tea, and the more delicate Lapsang Souchong.

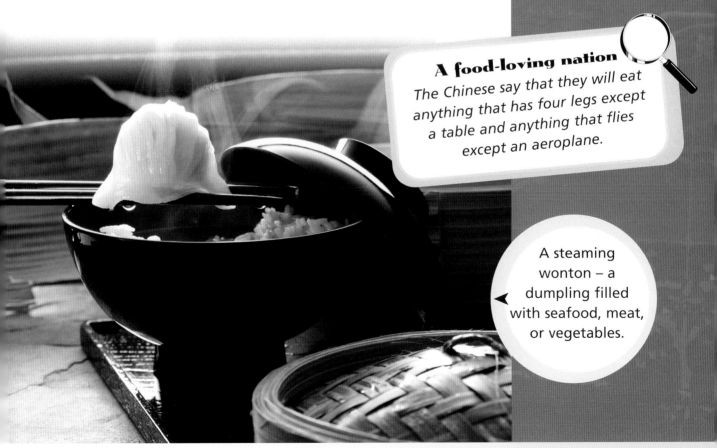

A food-loving nation
The Chinese say that they will eat anything that has four legs except a table and anything that flies except an aeroplane.

A steaming wonton – a dumpling filled with seafood, meat, or vegetables.

Religion in China

You have noticed many temples on your travels around China, but there is no official religion here. In fact, the Government banned it for a long time. Now, though, people are free to follow their own beliefs.

Although not an organized religion – more a set of rules for living – many people follow Confucianism. Confucius lived about 3,000 years ago. He taught that people should love one another, rule without force or violence, and treat others as they themselves would like to be treated. His influence can still be felt today.

Ancestor worship

Most Chinese people honour and worship their **ancestors**, whatever their religion. People regularly visit their graves and leave things like soap for them. In return, they hope their ancestors will help them get a job or find the right marriage partner.

An elderly man lights incense in honour of his ancestors at their graveside.

A Buddhist temple in Kunming, in the **province** of Yunnan.

WORD BANK   ancestor person who you are descended from

Taoism is another important religion in China. "Tao" means "the way" – meaning that Tao is the path that people should follow. Buddhism was introduced to China from India over 2,000 years ago and is followed by millions of people all over China, but especially in Tibet. Islam came to China from Central Asia, and today there are about four million Chinese Muslims. **Missionaries** brought Christianity to China in the early 17th century.

The exact numbers of people following different religions in China is not known. It was banned for so many years that even now, people are still reluctant to say that they follow a religion.

Fast fact
China has more than 13,000 Buddhist temples.

Yin and Yang
Yin and Yang are part of Taoism. Yang is everything in the world that is hot, hard, and masculine, often represented by the colour white. Yin is dark and hidden and feminine, and is often represented by the colour black. These forces have to be balanced to live in perfect harmony.

The Yin and Yang symbols represent harmony and order in the world. Yin is dark and Yang light.

missionary person who goes to other countries to do religious work

Wildlife & environment

Animals

There are more than 2,000 species of **terrestrial vertebrates**, 1,189 species of birds, 500 species of mammals, 210 species of **amphibians**, and more than 320 species of reptiles in China. Mammals include snow leopards, elephants, wild yaks, reindeer, bears, and tigers.

There are now only 1,600 pandas left in the wild. About 1,000 more are under protection in zoos and reserves.

Back in Beijing you decide to visit the zoo. Your favourite animal is the Giant Panda and this is one of the few places you can see one. It is China's most famous animal, and only eats bamboo. Bamboo trees are being cut down and used for scaffolding for the building industry and to make furniture. This makes it difficult for pandas to continue to live in the wild.

Animals and plants

The range of different animals and plants in China is among the greatest in the world. Some of the country's most famous animals are threatened with **extinction**. The places in which they live and the food they eat are being destroyed by China's rapid development.

WORD BANK amphibian animal such as a frog that lives both in the water and on the land
extinction no longer existing

Environmental issues

China has serious environmental problems. Forests are being cut down. Once land has no trees on it, it is easy for water to wash the soil away and for wind to blow it away. This is called erosion and it can cause serious flooding, as well as ruining the land for farming. It can also create deserts. Burning coal to produce electricity, and the rapid increase in the number of cars pollute the air.

The Government is planting trees all over China and is introducing more controls to stop as much pollution as possible.

China's beautiful landscapes are at risk of being ruined by pollution and other environmental problems.

Pollution

China relies on burning coal to produce its energy, and this produces a thick, unhealthy, polluting smog over many cities. Chongqing is nicknamed "Fog City" because of the pollution.

terrestrial vertebrate animal that has a backbone and lives on land

Stay or go?

You have been very lucky to have this quick glimpse of China, especially at a time when it is changing so quickly. There is still plenty to see and do, so what will you do – stay or go?

Still to see and do

- Shanghai's brand-new Formula One racetrack.
- The huge army of **terracotta** warriors that guard the tomb of the country's first emperor, Qin Shihuang. There are over 10,000 figures and chariots.
- A three-day cruise down the Chang Jiang from Chongqing to Wuhan.
- The caves at Longgong in Guizhou, which extend through 20 mountains.
- The white pagodas and stone forest water festivals and temples of Yunnan **Province** – and the occasional earthquake!
- The Grand Canal, built in 495 BC, which links the Hua He and Chang Jiang rivers, is the longest artificial river in the world.

China in space

After China's first astronaut came back from space in October 2003, he said he was unable to see the Great Wall of China from space. This is something schoolbooks have claimed for years. China was the third country, after the United States and Russia, to put an astronaut into space.

Yang Liwei, China's first astronaut, steps out of his capsule after his trip into space.

WORD BANK   terracotta type of clay

The amazing terracotta army, near Xi'an.

Thousands of tourists every year now travel through Pudong, one of Shanghai's two international airports.

A tourist hotspot

According to the World Tourism Organization, China will be the world's number-one tourist destination by 2020. The Government now also allows Chinese tourists to travel to the United Kingdom and Europe. Until recently, only businessmen could do this.

Find out more

World Wide Web

If you want to find out more about China you can search the Internet using keywords such as these:

- China
- Beijing
- Chang Jiang River

You can also find your own keywords using headings or words from this book. Try using a search directory such as www.google.co.uk

Films

Crouching Tiger, Hidden Dragon (2000)

Directed by Ang Lee, the film tells the story of a warrior's search for his stolen magical sword.

Destination Detectives can find out more about China by using the books and visiting the websites listed below.

The Chinese Embassy

The Chinese Embassy in your own country has lots of information about China. You can find out about the different regions, the best times to visit, special events, and Chinese culture.

The UK embassy website address is: www.chinese-embassy.org.uk

Further reading

The following books are packed with lots of useful information about China:

The Changing Face of China, Stephen Keeler (Hodder Wayland, 2002)

Cities of the World: Beijing, Deborah Kent (Children's Press, 1996)

Countries of the World: China, Carole Goddard (Evans Brothers, 2004)

Country File: China, Michael March (Franklin Watts, 2003)

Eyewitness: Ancient China, Arthur Cotterell, Alan Hills, and Geoff Brightling (Dorling Kindersley, 2000)

Nations of the World: China, Catherine Field (Raintree, 2003)

World Tour: China, Noelle Morris (Raintree, 2003)

Timeline

1600–1027 BC
Shang dynasty.
Beginning of a
writing system.

1027–221 BC
Zhou dynasty.
Confucius's lifetime.
Iron is used to make
tools for the first time
in China.

221–207 BC
Qin dynasty. Great Wall
of China is begun.
Emperor Ch'in is buried
with an army of
terracotta warriors.

206 BC–AD 220
Han dynasty.
Establishment of the
Silk Road and trading
with the West.

AD 220–420
Three Kingdoms and
Chin dynasty

AD 420–478
Song dynasty.

AD 581–618
Sui dynasty.

AD 618–907
Tang dynasty. Wu Chao
rules as empress for
45 years.

AD 960–1279
Song dynasty. Traders
begin sailing to south-
east Asia and India.

1280–1368
Yuan dynasty. Mongols
from the north invade
and take over China.

1368–1644
Ming dynasty. Work
begins on the Imperial
Palace.

1644–1911
Qing dynasty. China's
population begins to
rise rapidly.

1839–1842
War with Britain.

1900
The Boxer Rebellion: a
revolt against foreign
influence in China.

1911
Qing dynasty is
overthrown.

1911–1949
Republic of China:
many revolts and
occupation by
the Japanese.

1949
People's Republic of
China is established.

1966–1976
The Cultural
Revolution. During this
time schools are closed
and young people are
encouraged to rebel
against the system.

1976
Mao Zedong dies.

1978
Beginning of
economic reforms.

1989
Demonstration in
Tiananmen Square.

1997
Britain returns Hong
Kong to China.

2001
China awarded
the 2008 Summer
Olympic Games.

China – facts & figures

The red in China's flag symbolizes revolution. The large star represents the ruling Communist Party and the smaller stars represent the Chinese people.

People and places

- Population: 1.3 billion.
- Average life expectancy: men – 71; women – 74.
- In China, a person's surname comes first, followed by their given name, so Mao Zedong is Mr Mao not Mr Zedong.
- The lowest point in China is the Turpan Pendi basin, in the northwest. It is 154 metres (505 feet) below sea level.

Technology boom

- There are more mobile phones in China than land lines (269 million mobiles and 263 million land lines in 2003).
- In the next five years it is estimated that 178 million more people will buy a computer.

China's industry

- Major crops: rice, potatoes, sorghum, peanuts.
- Natural resources: coal, iron ore, crude oil, mercury, tin.
- Major industries: iron, steel, coal.
- The world's biggest shoe factory is in Guangdong province and employs 80,000 people.

Glossary

amphibian animal such as a frog that lives both in the water and on the land

ancestor person you are descended from

arable land that is suitable for cultivation

autonomous being separate or able to govern a region independently

BC stands for "Before Christ"

climate regular pattern of weather in an area

Communist person who follows a political belief system that calls for a classless society, where nobody owns anything and resources belong to a community

contour curved shape of a hill

drought temporary shortage of water

dynasty series of rulers from the same family

Equator imaginary line around Earth

ethnic group people with the same culture or nationality

extinction no longer existing

fertile land that is good for growing crops

floodplain area that floods when river water rises

funding money given to an organization for a particular purpose

growing season period when it is warm enough for crops to grow

gunpowder explosive powder used to shoot bullets from guns

hydroelectric electricity created by moving water

limestone rock created from the remains of sea animals

Mandarin official language of China

manufacturing making things from raw materials

martial art type of unarmed self-defence, often practised as a sport

meditating method of concentrating to calm the mind and body

metro rail system in an urban area

missionaries people who go to other countries to do religious work

municipalities main cities in China that have the same status as provinces

peasant poor person who lived and worked off the land

plateau area of high, flat land

port where ships load and unload cargo

preserved stopped from decaying or spoiling

province region that has its own local government

reform change made by the Government to improve the country

rural relating to the countryside

self-sufficient able to produce enough food for the population

silt fine particles of sand and rock carried and then deposited by a river

terrace step or ledge cut into a hillside

terracotta type of clay

terrain an area of land

terrestrial vertebrate animal that has a backbone and lives on land

tropical anything to do with the region either side of the Equator

turbine engine powered by water, steam, gas, or air

typhoon storm with very strong winds

urban relating to a city or built-up area

Index

air travel 9, 18
ancestor worship 38

Beijing 4, 5, 6, 7, 8, 9, 10, 11, 14, 18, 19, 20, 22, 25, 37, 40
Buddhism 6, 38, 39

calligraphy 23
Chang Jiang River 6, 12, 13, 42
Chengdu 27
Chongqing 7, 13, 19, 41, 42
cities 20–27
climate 10, 12, 29
Communism 6, 16
Confucianism 6, 38
Crouching Tiger, Hidden Dragon 31
culture 34
currency 6

Dong Xiaoping 17

emperors 8, 11, 16, 37, 42
environment 13, 40–41
ethnic groups 34–35

families 30, 34
farming 12, 28–29, 31, 33, 41
floods 10, 12, 16, 41
food 20, 28, 29, 32, 37
Forbidden City 8
Four Modernizations 17

Giant Panda 40
Gobi Desert 7
Government 6, 7, 8, 9, 30, 33, 35, 38, 41, 43
Great Wall of China 14, 42
Guangzhou 19, 26, 27
Guizhou 6, 42

Han 34
Harbin 10, 27
Himalayas 12

history 14-17
holidays 18, 36
Hong Kong 7, 18, 26
Hu Jintao 17
Huang He River 12, 42
Huangpu River 20
hutongs 25

Imperial Palace 14
Internet 24
inventions 14
Islam 39

Jing An Park 22

language 6, 34
Little Red Book 16
Long March, The 16
Longgong 42

Macau 7
Maglev train 21
mah jong 30
Manchu 34
Manchuria 11
Mandarin 4, 6, 34
Mao Zedong 16, 17
Ming dynasty 15
Mongolian 34
Mount Everest 7

New Year 4, 5, 37

Olympic Games 9
Oriental Pearl Tower 20, 21

paddy fields 28
peasants 8, 14, 15
People's Republic of China 8, 17, 36
population 6, 22, 25, 27, 28, 29
Pudong 20, 21

Qin dynasty 14
Qing dynasty 11, 15

Red Army 16
religion 6, 38–39
rural life 28–33

schools 22, 30, 32, 33, 34
seasons 10–11
Shanghai 7, 18, 20, 21, 22, 23, 24, 26, 42, 43
Shenzhen 7, 11, 26
Sichuan 37
Silk Road 15, 27
size of China 6
skiing 11
sport 36

Tai Chi 22
Taklimakan Desert 9, 15
Taoism 6, 39
tea 37
television 32
temperatures 7, 11
Temple of Heaven 4
Three Gorges Dam 13
Tiananmen Square 8, 17
Tianjin 7, 19, 26
Tibet 7, 39
Tibetan Plateau 7, 12
tourist attractions 31, 43-44
transport 18–19
Trans-Siberian Railway 18

Uygur 35

wildlife 28, 40
Worker's Stadium 36
World Financial Centre 21
writing 14, 33
Wuhan 42

Xi'an 27, 43
Xia dynasty 14

Yabuli 11
Yin and Yang 39
Yunnan 6, 38, 42

Zhuang 34

Titles in the *Destination Detectives* series include:

| Hardback | 1 406 20312 2 | Hardback | 1 406 20308 4 | Hardback | 1 406 20306 8 |

Hardback 1 406 20312 2

Hardback 1 406 20308 4

Hardback 1 406 20306 8

Hardback 1 406 20310 6

Hardback 1 406 20313 0

Hardback 1 406 20311 4

Hardback 1 406 20305 X

Hardback 1 406 20307 6

Hardback 1 406 20314 9

Find out about the other titles in this series on our website www.raintreepublishers.co.uk